Connemara's Walled Gardens

CLIFDEN AND ENVIRONS

GARY BROW

Design and typesetting by Jane Stark
seamistgraphics@gmail.com

ISBN 9789574059-0-5

Printed in Ireland by
KPS Colourprint Ltd. Knock, Co. Mayo

Ordnance Survey Maps
©Ordnance Survey Ireland/Government of
Ireland. Copyright Permit No. MP0006712

Thanks

This publication marks my family's appreciation of the late Joy and Rowan Blakeney
for their foresight in introducing us to Connemara and thanks to membership of the
Connemara Garden Club which gave me an entry passport to these gardens.
Everyone whom I approached for information or help, freely assisted me and truly
reflects the people from this part of the world's generosity to a relative stranger.

To my caring and thoughtful wife, Pearl,
and our wonderful daughters, Emily and Lydia

Holiday visits to Roundstone in the late 1960s made us aware of the necessity to bring along some provisions like garlic, wine and soft fruit which we knew were difficult to obtain there. We accepted this and in exchange enjoyed the food foraging for mushrooms, shellfish, hedgerow berries, pig nuts, herbs and seaweeds. Although all still available the graw for any east coast diet constituent is nowadays satisfied by multiple retail outlets and their choice in global products.

As we became more aware of Connemara's history and in particular the renovation of Kylemore Gardens it became apparent that exotic fruit, French wine and vegetables would have been easier procured as a guest of Mitchell Henry over a century earlier.

Then, with incidental mention to others and chance excursions, it became evident that there were a number of walled gardens that had been used for kitchen food production in the Clifden area. This along with personal attempts to create a productive garden and Clifden's bicentennial anniversary was the genesis of a notion to identify and look at, in a very primary fashion, these "other" gardens.

I hope the descriptions of them with their houses will give the reader a glimpse of their raison d'être.

The trend of growing your own food for whatever motivation (satisfaction, purity of produce, reduction of carbon footprint) is increasing and presents an opportunity for such abandoned gardens to be re-introduced to the 21st century.

Walled garden evolution

At some stage during the evolution from individual free foraging to cultivation, came the enclosure of a piece of land to mark ownership and protection. Later, separation from animal and human habitation occurred and the isolation of a growing area for food. Road and transport improvement then allowed travel and trade which encouraged larger areas of commercially grown produce, eventually leading to globalisation of production and sales.

These global growing areas in the past were subject to local open conditions of terrain and climate, each determining its predominant and frequently unique produce.

The world exploration period of the 16th and 17th centuries provided an opportunity for adventurers to bring home examples of this produce and passed them to the botanists to give the vegetative samples an identity and the challenge of reproduction outside their "natural environment".

The 19th century English period of industrial revolution and subsequent growth of individual wealth produced a change in life style, permitting estates with large houses. Household tastes became more cosmopolitan, with access to more exotic produce through the evolving trades of nurserymen and seedsmen. There was cheap labour for servicing all aspects of the household, ironwork availability with machinery and machined tools for water systems, heating and construction and horticulturists for agricultural advance. These "perfect storm conditions" of the Victorian period contributed to the creation of the walled garden for the confinement of fruit and vegetable production.

These grand high walled enclosures, laid out with strategically and methodically placed growing areas with individual climates, were accompanied by a large staff with dedicated jobs to manage the production of vegetables, fruit and flowers for the main house.

These same advances were similarly applied in Ireland, but with a great deal more modesty in the area of Connemara. The inclusion of such a garden benefited the owner in produce and in expressing his wealth and community status but would also target him in the country's future financial and social disruptions.

House and Garden selection

The Ballynahinch, Bunowen and Clifden castles in the early 19th century, were the largest household estates and had followed the distribution of land (by the Act of Settlement 1662) from the O'Flahertys. Their eventual debts and sale under the Encumbered Estates Acts 1848/9 (through the Encumbered Estates Court – EEC) was to be responsible for their division into smaller packages of land and offered at a "fire sale" price* to opportunistic buyers to build modern houses. This was one of the acts intended results, with the unltimate intention of populating the area, providing employment and improoving the land. Those who purchased were diverse in their background and motives.

At this time, observers of Connemara referred recurrently to its beauty, poverty, native language, perversity of inhabitants, dependance on the potato, poor roads and necessity for land improvement, particularly drainage. Those that purchased and accepted the challenge would have been aware of these observations but not, however of future events which were to include more crop failures (due to blight and weather), civil unrest (religious and political) and further land redistribution (Land Acts and Land League). This may go some way to explain why many of the houses had a high turnover of tenants or abandonment, or only apparently so as accuracy in owner-occupier identification is not clear as many on the census returns names may only have been renting. Two other points of note are that, today only two houses (Cleggan and Streamstown) remain in the original family tenancy, and there were a good number of marriages between members of different house holds in this area, presumably due to their social exposure within this limited wealthy group.

There would have been a great dependence on local food production for the occupants of these modest houses with their more cosmopolitan and educated diet; hence the inclusion of the walled garden in their home to provide suitable growing conditions for same. Labour was cheap and available at the time of house construction or improvement, with wealth reflected in the quality of build of these classified (according to the 1841 population census) "1st class" houses.

Identification of the house and garden for my observations centred around: its locality to Clifden; mapping on the 6 inch (1837-1842) and 25 inch (1888-1913) Ordinance Survey Ireland maps; the Galway County Councils list of Protected Structures.

Some houses identified under these criteria however turned out not to have a known walled garden and were: Abbey Glen Hotel (originally Glenowen orphanage), The Rectory (Clifden), Anglers Retreat (Toombeola), Roundstone Rectory, Ballinaboy House, Emlaghmore Lodge, Errisbeg House, Inagh Lodge, Kill House, Munga Lodge, Mission School (Ballyconneely), the Priory (Streamstown), Renvyle House, Rosleague Hotel, Rushnacurragh House.

Driving into Clifden my attention is often attracted to a number of gardens strips on their severe slope down to the harbour behind the Market and Post Office street houses. One in particular behind the Methodist building which has many walled garden features visible in early photographs, but is now less obvious.

Garden size and distance from house

The size of the examined gardens and houses varied considerably, but by dividing the individual garden area by it's house area (both measured on their OSI map, and the house area adjusted by its number of storeys), I had hoped to reveal a common ratio. Disappointingly, the results did not show any such significant relationship.

The distances between house and garden also showed great variations. A step for some (Garraunbaun) and a long stroll or carriage ride for others (Kylemore

Methodist church 1900s (Courtesy of the National Library of Ireland)

Methodist church 2012 (right)

gardens), but in practical terms a kitchen garden should be as close to the kitchen as possible. However the terrain, orientation, size and householder choice may have influenced otherwise but gardens of these very modest sized houses and land dictated a short distance from the main house. The luxury of a distant concealed kitchen garden, a feature of the Victorian Kylemore estate, required land, an army of supervised gardeners and good communications with the cook. It also afforded the householder and their guests an excursion from the house, and opportunity to show off this orderly lay out of vegetables, fruit and flowers.

The distance marked on the garden maps is measured in my paces with 1 pce=2.65feet=0.81 metres, and from the nearest garden gate to the rear of the house.

Orientation

A garden's orientation aims to capitalize on the available light and heat from the sun and protection afforded by natural or artificial shelter. Within this orientation different plants have priorities for positioning which place them in optimal positions to help them flourish.

There were patterns in these gardens that did confirm plant orientation.

Where fruit trees were found or known to have grown, they occupied mainly the western half of the garden, the wall supports for soft fruit were mainly on the south facing wall surface and similary the siting of glass houses.

My expectations were that the majority of gardens would have their long axis running east-west. However, reviewing their orientation, they were split, with only 50% having their long axis east-west and the remaining 32% sited north-south and 18% neither, due to their square configuration.

The discrepancies in expectations are not out of line with modern general expert advice. For example, on the siting of greenhouses, where the advice is divided between east-west and north-south orientation, and may be dependant on specific growing requirements if utilising the low morning spring sun or avoiding the full summer sun etc.

It is likely that the site and orientation of these gardens was individually chosen with consideration given to the amount and features of the land. These would have included distance from main house, land gradient, prevailing wind direction, shelter afforded and position to the sun for the type of crops to be grown.

Shelter and trees

Shelter belt trees reduce the force of the wind hitting the garden wall and also disturb its laminar flow and both these alterations reduce the wind speed and turbulance on the leeward side of the wall.

The houses and their gardens were at relatively low lying levels and don't usually present a snow or frost hazard but because of their coastal positions are all subject to wind and those closest to the coast, salt laden wind. This would have influenced the choice of shelter tree planted and undoubtedly many originally did not survive particulary those displaced from foreign parts. The 25 inch OSI map's characteristics clearly identify deciduous and coniferous trees planted around the majority of these walled gardens.

All the gardens visited had some visible mature tree wind shelter at this stage in their existance, some so much that they now almost obliterate the light to the gardens they once protected just from the wind. This is particulary obvious when the locations are viewed on Google Earth.

The predominant tree is the sycamore and some conifers, with these latter shallow rooted trees being most in evidence of recent falling. Birch comes next and usually in a sycamore mix planting along with ash. Oak is present but prominent only in Glendolagh and beech within the confines of concommitant shelter from other species. The copper variety frequently individually on an avenue or near the main house. Oaks frugality may possibly be explained by past mature timber harvesting (Kylemore and Glendolagh may have offered some resistance to the lumberjack) but beech, by its requirement of sheltered growing conditions. Other types (chestnut, cherry, lime) were observed but outside the shelter belt in isolated situations only.

The unattended and ungrazed walled gardens succumb to invasion by natural seed distribution, when the sally, ash and sycamore dominate and where the invasive rhododendron may reach tree sized proportion.

Walls

The stone walls viewed in these gardens varied somewhat from garden to garden. The principle constituent, granite stone, (the exception being the brick of Kylemore Gardens and part of Ballynahinch) was rarely cut (or faced) of mixed size and colour and sourced locally from the open ground or quarry.

All the walls were double, having an outer and inner stone with frequently smaller stones and mortar (core) in between and further strenghtened by a stone lying transversely with each end on a face, the "through and bond-stones". The lime and mortar for this binding "cement" was readily available, frequently from a nearby lime kiln and mortar pit. An occasional wall was totally dry stone (eg Kylemore House) with little core and found not to be durable nor of any great height.

There appeared a wider stone foundation at the base and the walls thickness diminished with increasing height (eg. the older Bunowen Castle's circular wall, Clifden Monastery) to be "capped" to help throw off water by a variety of finishes which was the clients choice. So too apparently their decision to have courses in the wall, which are described as a visually pleasing layer of stones laid to a set height.

Wall heights varied from garden to garden and sometimes within the same garden in different orientations, the higher usually being on the western walls. There appears from questioning little reason for the commoner 8 ft height but it is regarded as a practical height associated with stability due to proportionaly of

Garden wall

width and height and with no doubt consideration given to the necessity for scaffolding and the cost for additional height. Other reasons given for this height ranged from keeping people out, (I did read of a steward reporting to his superior during the famine time that the garden had been plundered), deer from jumping in (deer were more common in the mid-19th century Connemara), privacy for those inside (a Victorian code for the ladies visiting the herbacous border), and greater wind protection (which diminishes with increasing garden size).

The walls viewed had no additional supporting piers or buttresses but depended on this depth/height ratio to allow for their lasting stability. The exception is again Kylemore with its higher, lengthy walls where piers appear at regular intervals.

Apart from sections of wall collapse through accident of fallen timber etc., portions of walls were also missing or even dropped in height by stone removal for use elswhere, as the garden wall function or interest became less important.

Rendering is a layer of finer lime mortar applied to a wall resulting in a flat surface which may increase wall heat retention and does facilitate nail insertion. It was not a common finding but was found on some south facing walls (Kylemore Gardens, Shanboolard, Ballynahinch, Glendolagh) and one east facing (Cleggan) where the walls were used for fanning fruit trees or even lean to greenhouses.

Openings in the walls allowed passage of people and through the larger, carriage of materials by cart etc. Numbers and sites of these openings seem to

Iron nails in rendered wall

relate to passage of visitors (nearest the pathway to the house) and those of the gardeners (wider and nearer out buildings, manure or water source).

Undoubtedly all were gated (and even locked by the head gardener) and some elaboratly pillared (eg. Ballynahinch) or arched (egs Kylemore, Clifden castle).

A frequent feature of the walls (abandoned or otherwise) was their abundant growth of common ivy which may provide some water and heat repellant benefit to the wall and is also a usefull late feed for honey bees. When it's aerial roots invade and fragment the mortar it can also, by it's bulky sail like wind resistance, help lead to the wall's collapse. I cannot recall seeing any such collapse secondary to this ivy on my inspections, which might just be due to the integrity of the mortar, wind sheilding or just a phenomenon of an, as yet, inadequate time span.

The wall variations I found relate to cost, with the meanest procuring a simple low dry stone wall but on expenditure, increasing with mortar, courses, capping, height, faced stone and brick. The most obvious and modern example examined of the latter is that of Kylemore Gardens.

An ivy-covered wall

Lime Kilns

Lime kilns burnt lime stone (also sea shells or marble) to produce lime which was most commonly added to the soil to sweeten it (increase its ph), or combined with mortar for binding stones in construction. Their frequent finding nearby to these gardens is therefore not unexpected and of benefit to the gardener and stone mason alike.

An enclosed combustion chamber with flue is loaded with layers of lime stone and combustible material, ignited, the chamber sealed and the continued high temperature achieved over days turns the limestone to dry dust.

These structures vary little in principle and in places make use of the local terrain in their construction. The one assocated with the gardens of Glendollagh makes use of the lower area for combustion, and subsequently extraction, and at the higher level, flue and limestone loading. Others however may be constructed on the level like a small house, are well documented and scattered about Connemara.

Mortar

Lime, mixed with coarse sandy material and water, produces a tenacious mixture which dries slowly to a firm agent, to bind stones in position. This coarse sandy material is found in scattered pits (mortar pits) excavated for this purpose and the resultant sand/lime "cement" used in wall and house construction. A finer quality is obtained by removing (sifting) the coarser stones from the sandy material.

Its use in these garden walls incurs an additional cost but strengthens them, assisting height and stability with the non intentional but useful benefit of allowing nails to be held in the wall for plant support.

A mortar pit

Manure

The natural "soil" of Connemara's bog land is severely lacking in nutrients, expands with rain and contracts and compacts under drought conditions. The addition of manure into the land, greatly improves its fertility, texture and productivity. Rotted down horse, cattle, fowl, pig or sheep dung provided this along with the vast resources of seaweed from nearby shores.

From verbal history and deduced in originating from animals associated with the mapped out-houses, there was a ready source of manure for these gardens and doubtless the gardeners employed could have outsourced it if not readily available to them. I have heard contemporary use of the term "manuring" the land when referring to the commercially produced particulate form of plant nutrients which are applied, and must surely do little to improve Connemara's soil texture.

Drainage

Even visitors are aware of the strange water retentive property of bog land as they experience undulating movements whilst walking on it, view the many lakes within it, and hear frightening stories of people dissappearing into it. Fed by coastal rainfall and mountain run off, it predominates the many 19th centurys enigneering and agricultural reports in explaining the necessity for land drainage.

Not surprising then that nearly all the gardens are situated on a slope as a natural form of drainage and many have incorporated additional man made passages for water diversion.

The construction of French drains is known in many of the gardens where digging has revealed them and are often found under old garden pathways.

Streams passing throught the gardens in Ballynahinch and Clifden castle had been concealed underground in pipe or stone to reappear outside the garden. In Kylemore Gardens and Letterdyfe they flow through on the surface.

Diverting ditches are present outside the higher (north) wall of Errislannan and lower (north) wall of Crocnaraw and there is a culvert opening for water egress at the lower (south) end of Cartron.

Parallel streams flow down the ouside of the garden walls in Kylemore House and Glendolagh.

Where necessary all have apparently heeded the engineers and agriculturists advice, as I experienced no particular evidence of function failure under varying wet weather conditions, except in the south end of Ballynahinch.

The global rainfall pattern changes and increasing temperatures over the past one and a half centurys, fuel the complexities of climate change interpretation. The increased temperature and seasonal changes in rainfall predictated for Ireland appear geographical within the country.

Connemara, with its governing Atlantic maritime weather, may however escape the drought and enjoy some slight increase in temperature. An elderly

Clifden man, with whom I once sheltered under a vegetable stand awning which poured off rain, sucked on his pipe (the lit tobacco protected by a metal pipe cap), and pronounced that we were "cursed with the rain". His declaration may continue a valid criticism.

Water Supply

A lake, stream or well was never located far away from any of the gardens visited and by various means were harnessed to supply principally the house but also the garden. A common set up was water damed at a higher point or held in a holding tank to be run down to the garden or house in pipes, (Errislannan, Zetland, Letterdyfe, Kylemore House) or more simply, a diverting culvert used to fill a holding pond within the garden (Kylemore House).

For those houses and gardens sited above the open water level, an electrical pump was employed (Garraunbaun), and wells with potable water for the household are invariably found close to many established significant households (eg Crocnaraw, Roundstone monastery, Streamstown.)

With a very adequate head of pressure it was also possible to run a power tool via a turbine (Kylemore House and Kylemore Gardens).

Glasshouses

Mid-19th century saw iron foundaries flourish with the industrial revolution and along with the glass tax relaxation helped induce the mass production of glass houses. Previously the lean to greenhouse, used the reflective and radiating heat of its associated wall, but was superceeded (by those that could afford it) by new free standing greenhouses. The furnaces used in the larger estates in the past to heat the walls could now be placed distant from the greenhouse and by various elaborate methods used to heat many areas. All this ultimately produced a new controllable enviroment for exotic plant and fruit growth which helped fill the demands from the new finds of the foreign returned.

There were disappointingly few findings that glasshouses had any great uptake in these gardens I visited in Connemara.

Mitchell Henry, however, incorporated many of the glass house revolutionary arrangements which were available to him at this time and are perhaps visually better understood in many of their current unrestored exposed state.

The remainder of the gardens visited only revealed a few greenhouse remnants (Shanboolard, Letterdyfe, Southhill), and Lisnabruka with the remains of a furnace and Ballynahinch which has an almost intact one for the hot bed it serviced.

Today's appearance of polytunnels in the grounds of houses could well be interpreted as the relatively inexpensive adaptation and provision of a walled garden. The incongruity in some of their site choice induces criticism which will hopefully encourage future thoughtful consideration for their aesthetic positioning.

Bee-keeping

This would seem a reasonable additional facility for a walled garden to have nearby for pollination. Their existance in these gardens is difficult to confirm as hives disintegrate with time especially the 19th century straw constructed skeps. In addition it may have been considered imprudent to site the hive within the garden.

Boles however were recesses in walls in which these skeps were placed for weather protection, usually south facing and were of a variable shape, size and number and are historical physical evidence of bee keeping. There were only two possible single boles found on these garden examinations, Derrigimlagh and Crocknaraw.

Crocknaraw (*page 11, left)* is deemed too shallow (12"H x 13"W x 8"D) to house a skep and also appears to have been either a blocked up window in an

altered wall, or a shelf for tools, religious object, lamp or gardeners lunch.

The Derrigimlagh recess (*page 11, right*) (14"H x 12"W x 12"D) however, is considered a bee bole and is now recorded as such in the International Bee Research Association, Bee Bole Register (No. 1525).

Questioning people associated with the gardens, who had recent (20th century) past knowledge, do recall bees being kept in: Cleggan House (outside garden mid-20th century), Southhill (1930-1950), Roundstone Monastery (until 1960s), Crocnaraw (late 20th century), Zetland (late 20th century), Kylemore Gardens (probably yes, but not known where), Ballynahinch (mid-20th century), Shanboolard (currently, but at a distance from garden).

Today, with the exception of Shanboolard, none of the gardens have bee keeping associated with them and probably reflects the disuse of the gardens and their horticulture, greater commercial availablity of honey and loss of bee management, rather than a dissapearance of bees.

Despite the current challenge to bee keepers (mites, viruses, colony collapse) it is encouraging to know that there is an immediate past history of sustainability for bee keeping in this area and with the re-emergence of growing your own food, that bee keeping too is experiencing a renaissance. (Connemara Beekeepers' Association)

Icehouses

Ice houses were present mid-18th century in Ireland and associated with the largest of households principally for food preservation and cooling table foodstuffs. They were purpose built chambers to store ice, often partly subterranean, roofed, with drainage at their base, an entrance door for extraction and usually another higher for insertion of the ice. Sited in different areas of the estate to suit the structural requirements, often shaded by surrounding trees, and managed by the gardener and house steward. More elaborate entrances, forms of insulation and roofing all incorporated into a garden architectural feature, do exist in Ireland but those found here were basic.

Ice sources were from local frozen fresh water lakes (often dirty and inconsistent), imported ice (from as far afield as America, Norway, Russia) or delivered by the "ice man" from Dublin ice importers. It is unlikely that the western seaboard climate had persistent winter frozen lake conditions to support a lake source for the Connemara ice houses and it was suggested to me that ice for the Ballynahinch ice house came in to Clonisle pier at Toombeola, from Norway.

The larger capacity Ballynahinch ice house may relate not so much to the households demand but that of the salmon industry (fresh fish and canning factory) associated with the river and/or its export via train or boat.

The Kylemore Castle estate ice house (in Kylemore Farm, formally Addergoole Farm) is a long distance from the Castle is smaller but with the essential basics. It's simple construction seems likely attributable to it's former owner (Eastwood of Addergoole Farm) for the farm household's use rather than Mitchell Henry's whose requirements, if constructed, I imagine would have been greater and more elaborate. There is a construction at the Kylemore lakeside (and passed on the walk-way to the Abbey) of a long stone built chamber with an arched bricked roof and 4 circular roof openings. It is covered in earth with mature trees now, entered by a simple door and referred to currently as an old "coal" store but an early 20th century staff member remembers it as a "cold" store associated with fish from the estate. Ice house construction was dissappearing in the 19th century as refridgeration evolved by other means and undoubtedly the Henry estate would have been up to date on this.

The possible ice house at Mallmore is only categorised as a possible due to its partial subterrainian north facing site and inner arched brick roof but it has an incongruous number of windows and entrances.

Kylemore Farm ice house

Ballynahinch interior with blocked up loading window at road end.

Past Garden Planting

Needless to say I found no cabbages or turnips in these long since cultivated gardens and in the more recently unattended, only scattered blackcurrant, raspberry and a few fruit trees.

The absence of really old fruit trees within the gardens is easily explained by their natural expected life span of 30 to 50 years along with their susceptibility to disease. Where they were present, they were within the lifetime of local knowledge and most frequently pear and apple and near a wall.

I was not aware in any of the gardens visited of any evidence of past potato ridges and imagine potatoes would not have warranted a space in this prime growing area, being grown outside the walled garden or out sourced.

There was therefore little or no evidence of past planting and only Errislannan Manor and Kylemore Gardens have known records of planting lists and varieties. Apart from these, assumptions can only be made from general seed catalogues for the time.

Background reading for these gardeners to look for presumptive evidence of garden produce from any meal description yielded very little, describing only the meat rather than their vegetable or fruit content.

Pantry diaries or for example the export inventory from Kylemore Gardens might help investigation of garden produce details, but would command very specific research to yield confident results.

Kylemore Abbey 'cold' house

Kylemore Abbey 'cold' house entrance

Ballynahinch entrance

The Gardens

Garden drawing symbols

Symbol	Description	Symbol	Description
N ↑	Direction of North	·····	Pathway
▬▬▬	Stone wall	→► 24 pcs.	No of paces to house
▬ ▬	Wall with opening/gate	⑧	Wall height (feet)
∿∿	Broken wall	▭	Building
▷─▷	Slope of ground	☘	Deciduous tree/named
∿∿∿	Stream and flow direction	⚚	Coniferous tree

Townland: This is the townland in which the house associated with the garden is located.

GPS: These coordinates are different from the "Grid reference".

These are the Global Positioning System (satelite navigation) coordinates which can be entered in the "Search/Fly to" box in Googleearth and will take you directly to the garden.(Some views are obliterated by cloud – try the "Historical imagery" in "View" or the "Ortho" view in OSI maps.)

Elevation: Metres above sea level of the garden.

Access: Permission to access a garden may be obtained from the associated house where identifed (e.g., Hotel) and respected as not permitted when identified as Private.

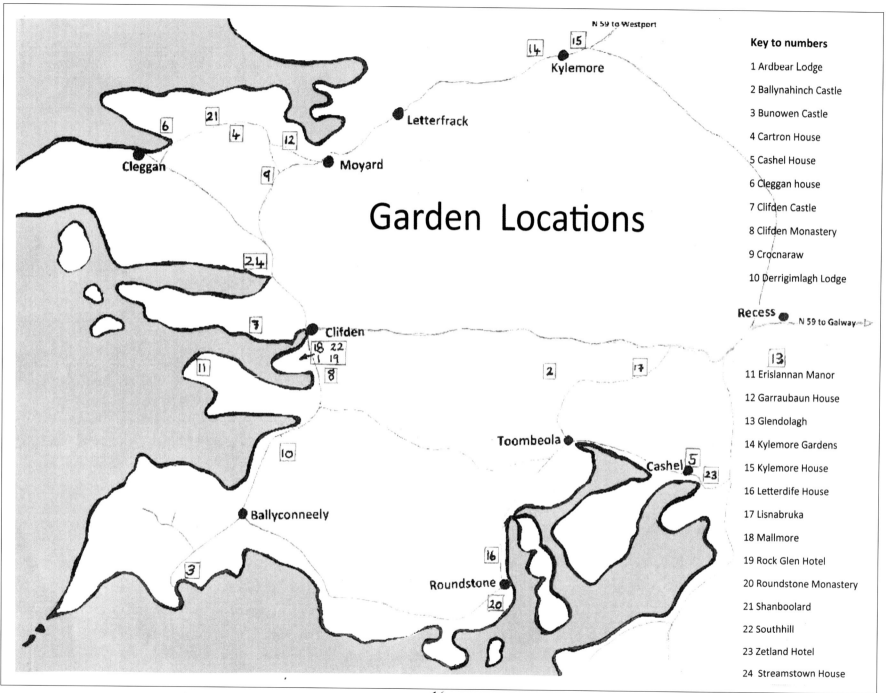

Garden Locations

Key to numbers

1 Ardbear Lodge
2 Ballynahinch Castle
3 Bunowen Castle
4 Cartron House
5 Cashel House
6 Cleggan house
7 Clifden Castle
8 Clifden Monastery
9 Crocnaraw
10 Derrigimlagh Lodge
11 Erislannan Manor
12 Garraubaun House
13 Glendolagh
14 Kylemore Gardens
15 Kylemore House
16 Letterdife House
17 Lisnabruka
18 Mallmore
19 Rock Glen Hotel
20 Roundstone Monastery
21 Shanboolard
22 Southhill
23 Zetland Hotel
24 Streamstown House

Townland:	Ardbear
GPS:	53° 28' 43" N 10° 01' 34" W
Elevation:	28m
Protected Structure:	No
Access:	Private

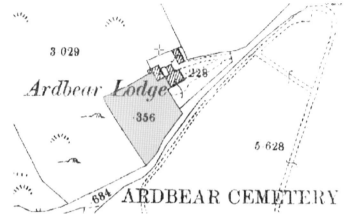

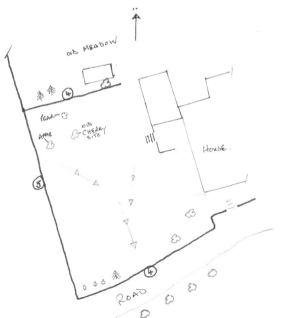

Ardbear Lodge

This smallish residence known now as Ardbear Lodge appears to have been named differently when built by Duane circa 1826 as a home (This more recent name may have lead to some confusion in its recorded history, being mistaken for the Ardbear lodge, a protected structure, and associated with Ardbear House). It was bought by Jones in 1839 who leased it to a number of people before being sold again through the EEC.

Following its sale in the mid-1860s recorded owners were Connolly, Emerson and in 1985 to date McLoughlin, with little structural changes over the years except for a southern extension.

Little by way of outhouses and the walled garden sits in a natural sheltered and sloping hollow on the western side of the house. A similar sized adjacent plot north of the northern wall was referred to as the meadow. Known vegetable marketing took place during the Emerson occupation and their garden skills transferred to Cashel House through daughter Kay McEvilly. The garden until quite recently had a large cherry (probably non-fruiting like a number in the area) pear and apple trees with some replanting taken place, but currently this garden is in lawn.

View N to S

View NNE to SSW

View S to N

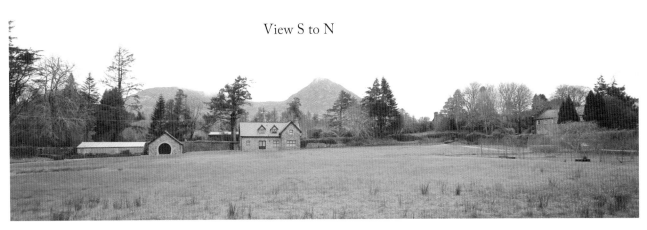

Townland:	Ballynahinch
GPS:	53° 27' 37" N 9° 51' 52" W
Elevation:	19m
Protected Structure:	Yes
Access:	At hotel

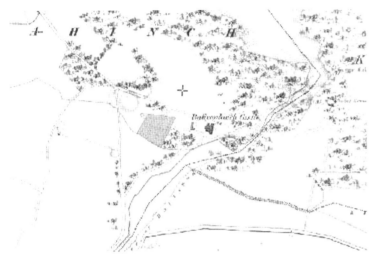

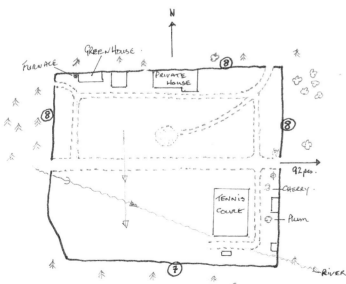

Ballynahinch Castle

At the turn of the 19th century the Martin family occupied this landmark building from where the extensive estate was managed. Under the EEC, the Ballynahich estate was sold to the Law Life Assurance Company (1852) before the castle and some of the estate was purchased by the Berridge Family (1872) and then the Indian cricketer Ranjitsinkji (1933). It has subsequently been owned by McCormack, the Irish Tourist Board, Huggard, Ball, and currently Mason, with its formalisation into a hotel in 1946.

The large walled garden is shown as well laid out in the 6 inch map, with orderly pathways and growing sections with little shown associated tree shelter. This early order and picture of specific growing areas is supported by recent findings of subterranean stream drainage from west to east across its southerly sloping aspect. Continuing interest in the gardens development was a later introduction of a heated greenhouse on the west end of the north wall and the inclusion of a gardener's house complete with the gardener's summoning bell beside it. This house was converted to a school for the Berridge family and is now a private house (1990) with an even more recent addition (2009) of a stone shed but the bell has since dissappeared. The garden outline has been altered in the north west corner and red brick replaces the inner stone facing between the current greenhouse and new build house. The south west wall was more recently altered to facilitate building development. Substantial tree planting and growth has occured since the early map.

Apart from the structural artefacts and good condition walls with some supportive iron nails in the north wall, there remains little evidence of past garden planting, apart from an elderly (but not ancient) cherry and plum tree inside the east wall. None of the gardens original pathways remain laid out, except that between the east and west main pillared entrances. A tennis court was introduced in the 1980s in the south east corner and more recently some small animal housing.

Todays usage of the garden varies from temporary event location, some occasional soft fruit and vegetable growing with plant propagation in the greenhouse, but mainly it is grassed and fallow, offering a commercial garden produce opportunity to support the hotels kitchen.

View NE to SW

Townland:	Bunowenmore
GPS:	53° 24' 55" N 10° 06' 32" W
Elevation:	7m
Protected Structure:	No
Access:	Private

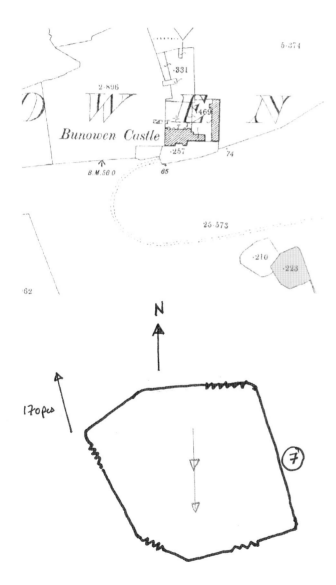

Bunowen Castle

The castle's origin in the 13th century was associated with many of Connemara's rulers, in particular, its most notorious, Grace O'Malley, through her marriage to its owner Donal O'Flaherty. Mid-16th century the castle was forfeited to Geoghegan whose descendants in 1756 changed the castle's site to its current higher northern position. Following bankruptcy it was bought by Blake through the EEC, but his unfinished work led to the Congested Districts Board purchasing it in 1909 with land distribution to its previous tenants.

This derelict castle sits silhouetted against the skyline, surrounded by a large apron of bare ground and grazing sheep. The 6 inch map shows a walled area just to its north west with pathways and regular plantings but there is no local knowledge of this being a walled kitchen garden and the walls are all low in keeping with a field boundary wall. There are no sheltering trees here or anywhere near this weather exposed area and it is unlikely it was used for kitchen garden purposes, but more likely potato or grain crops.

The maps also show two attached enclosing walled areas to the south of the castle which were presented to me as walled gardens. They are shown near the shore line, in the shelter of Doon hill to the west and the more western one on the 6 inch map has a small enclosed building. However, on inspection only the eastern one remains which has substantive walls and along with its shape and height certainly suggest more than field walls. Today it functions as an animal enclosure which is, perhaps, a clue as to their original purpose.

View N to S

East gate entrance

Culvert exit under south wall

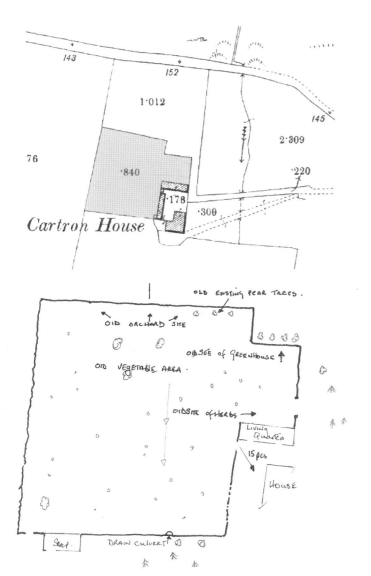

Cartron House

A house with close geographical and family connections to Shanboolard Hall. Cartron House was another build on a fine site by the astute Joseph Reville(Nimmo's pay clerk) in the early 19th century with land acquired on a lease from Robert Graham and where the Revilles were to live. With intervening owners (Goreham *et al*) Cartron house was eventually bought by William and Kate Armstrong-Lushington-Tulloch of Shanboolard (sister-in-law of Robert Graham) in the early 20th century and where Kate went to live after the second world war following the death of her second husband and until her own death in 1938. One of her great-grandchildren, Ann Goodbody, inherited Cartron then subsequently her daughter Nichola Musgrave (Cleggan House), and whose family are now renovating the house and grounds.

The garden immediately adjacent on the west side of the house has a gentle slope towards the lake and enclosed by lowish walls, the western one being of stone and earth variety (moot wall). On the west are open fields and the south offers some shelter by conifers and on the north by sycamores. There is no obvious local water source although a stream has a course through the house grounds and the modern source is pumped from the lake. Drainage evidence is from a culvert below the southern wall. Despite the presence of outhouses these were not known to house domestic animals.

The gardens are remembered in the 20th century, when six gardeners worked between Shanboolard and Cartron . On entering through the east side gate there was an unheated greenhouse on the right, raised herb beds on the left with the main vegetable crops occupying the remainder of the enclosed area, and apple and pear trees across the northern area.

The lean periods of permanent occupancy in the latter part of the 20th century led to the gardens disuse and ultimately total neglect. It presented a hazard to this curious visitor seeking to view and measure the interior, who had to retreat, defeated by the dense uncontrolled fertility. Perhaps it may be reclaimed via the keen gardener Kate Armstrong-Lushington-Tulloch's 21st century's genes.

Townland:	Cashel
GPS:	53° 25' 10" N 9° 48' 23" W
Elevation:	19m
Protected Structure:	Yes
Access:	At hotel

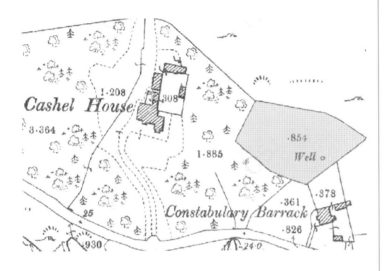

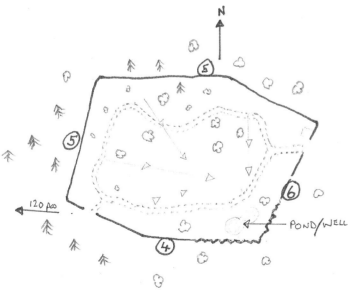

Cashel House

This 2 storey house was built for Thomas Hazell in the 1840s in an area of known mild coastal climate conditions, permitting his wife to carry out much decorative planting and Thomas to be at the collective centre of his business as a kelp buyer. The following owner James O'Mara TD (circa 1920) allowed his botany interests convert the map charachterised walled orchard area to the east of the house (seen on 6 inch map) to plant imported rare trees and in so doing lowering some of the stone walls. The following owner Lt Col Brian Clayton (1952) added Fuchsia collections to the garden and the latest garden lovers, McEvilly, bought the house and opened it as a hotel in 1968.

The hotel with all its extensions and updates has not sacrificed any of its splendid garden architecture or content, rather adding to it by giving its guests the unexpected pleasure of virtually all year round colour in its microclimate.

Despite the absence of any significant past or present evidence of the walled garden area being used for vegetable production, the current owners have responded to the needs of the house's change in usage and kitchen demands with a vegetable plot along a garden walkway to the sheltered west of the hotel.

Walled orchard

View N to S

North stone and earth wall (moot)

Outside western wall

Inside western wall

Townland:	Cleggan
GPS:	53° 33' 43" N 10° 06' 08" W
Elevation:	17m
Protected Structure:	Yes
Access:	Private

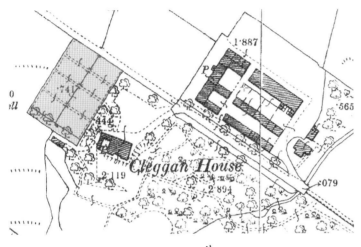

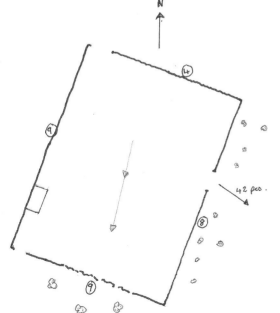

Cleggan House

An engineer, Fred Twining (Tea importers, UK) purchased the land from the Martins encumbered estate with the intention of building a model farm and the 25 inch map confirms the farm buildings, house and also a walled garden and history confirming his success. Cleggan House has remained owned by a blood relative to the present day. Although with varied past usage, the house is now a permanent private residence and the outlying farm housing, although no longer part of its domain, its ownership also remains within the family's lineage.

The garden slopes gently down to the south and mature planted shelter, the paths marked on the plan of the symmetrical garden and once discovered stone drains are no longer visible and there are surprisingly treeless open fields on the exposed side of the western wall. This wall has a strip of rendering half-way up and some unusual ventilation holes on the western side of the south wall which housed pigs on the other side.

The gardens worked history became inconsistent as only seasonal occupancy of the house dictated its attention. The last known active management was by the current owners grandfather on his return from a prisoner of war camp in 1945 with family memories of fanned plums on the walls, apple trees, vegetables and also surprisingly flowers which were sold to the Clifden hotels. The walls except for a portion of the south wall remain intact but the north wall was never known to be higher than about 4 feet, of stone and earth combination type constituting a moot wall.

The garden ground is now partly fenced, clean and grassed but devoid of any past growing history save for some eye nails in the part rendered western wall. Some raised beds, kennels and occasional livestock containment serve the familys needs today.

Track through stables

View NW to SE

South wall gate

Townland:	Clifden Demesne
GPS:	53° 29' 34" N 10° 03' 37" W
Elevation:	51m
Protected Structure:	Yes
Access:	Private

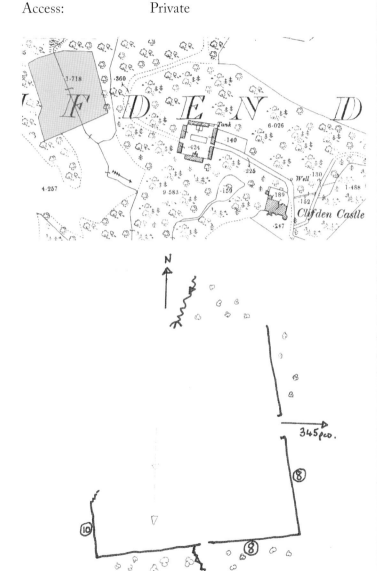

Clifden Castle

The Protected Structure's website refers to this as a sham castle but viewed by the historically challenged eyes of this visitor, it appears to contain all the mystical and romantic features of a real castle. Built by John D'Arcy for himself and his large family as he translocated from Kiltullagh in the early 19th century (1812-1818) to Clifden as it became established.

Following crop failures, famine and death of this considerate landlord, town developer and magistrate, he left the castle to his son Hyacynth until the 1847 famine consequences resulted in its sale through the EEC to the Eyre family from Bath. Although some structural investment changes were made the castle did not continue as a full time home and its intermittent occupation by the Eyres ultimately led to its abandonment and land distribution to tenants by the Land Commission. The Castle remains an intriguing site especially from the sea and also gazing into its interior where there is still sufficient structure to imagine a once large vibrant family 3 storeyed home.

The walled garden lies to the west at the end of a track which runs from the house through the extensive stable yard with living accomodation, then uphill to the entrance through an arched gateway. The walls remain in very good repair on the east, south and south west corner, but the remainder no longer exist, leaving the once enclosed garden continuous with the now bare adjacent fields which rise up to the west and whose boundaries themselves are well outlined in stone walls. Small trees on the north east, east and south give some shelter to the garden as it slopes down towards the sea. A stream marked as running down through it, is now piped underground on this clean fallow ground.

View W to E

Entrance pillars on west

North Wall

Townland:	Ardbear
GPS:	53° 28' 46" N 10° 01' 04" W
Elevation:	7m
Protected Structure:	No
Access:	Private

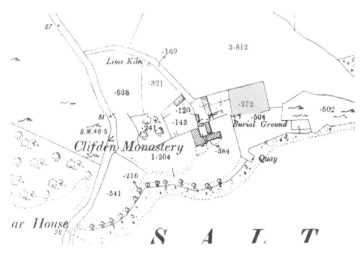

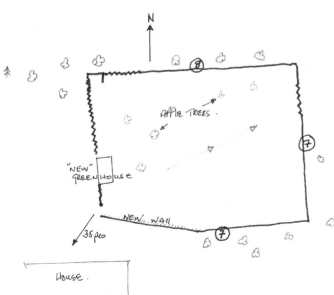

Clifden Monastery

The Franciscans were in Clifden Quay House in 1837 and moved into a house on their current site overlooking the Salt Lake in 1844 or 1853. From the 6 inch map it appears there was a garden already in existence possibly established by Mr Brown its previous owner/ occupier. This purchase would have been a tactical move by Archbishop McHale who opposed National Schools and to counteract the prosletysing by Church Mission schools, to establish the brothers in a teaching capacity and built their school nearby to the north, on the now disused pottery site. At this time financial support from the brothers' administrative centre in Mountbellew was poor and this school had to be self supporting for the brothers and to feed the school children. The farm animals and garden produce would reflect this along with monies from the sale of their goods locally (milk up until the 1960s). Local fishing and fowling rights added to the brothers larder as indeed did the Letterfrack Ellis Quakers with their ecumencial food donations to the monastery for children during the great famine. Nearby Samuel Jones's private residence, Ardbear House, was taken over as a school by the Franciscans in 1875.

A church and a two storey outbuilding were later added to this working farm of 17 acres, and demolition of the house and a new build completed in 1978.

With the schools reversion to lay teachers and diminution in brothers' numbers, the monastery has seen a reduction in their scholastic and pastoral involvement to the point where the farm became no longer necessary and the garden was last worked 15 years ago.

The garden lies close at hand slightly below to the north-east in a sloping hollow, sheltered to the west by rising ground with planted conifers and the north by a line of sycamores. Parts of the west, north and east walls have fallen, and the south west corner was claimed for accomodation and car parking at the rear of the house. A few old apple trees within the west and north side of the garden offer little resistance to advancing brambles and soft fruits gone wild, but this overgrowth is not yet sufficiently established for it to be despised.

View SW to NE

East garden

East garden (north-east corner)

Outside north wall

The west garden

Townland:	Crocnaraw
GPS:	53° 32' 36" N 10° 00' 25" W
Elevation:	23m
Protected Structure:	No
Access:	At guesthouse

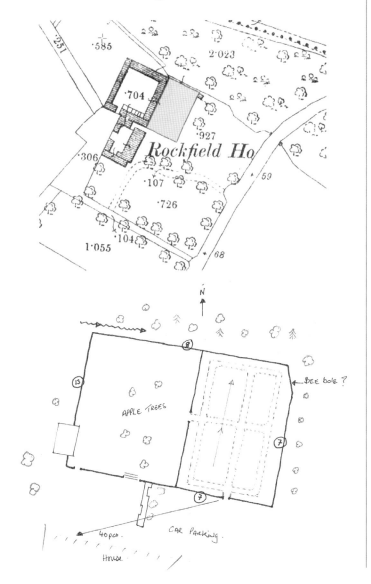

Crocnaraw

A house built in the early 1850s on land bought by Robert Graham in 1839 and leased to Thomas Butler. At one stage it was a protestant boys orphanage. Beresford Barrett, an Irish forester, later resided here and from whom the current owner Lucy Fretwell's parents bought the house in the 1960s.

The 25 inch map shows a well demarcated house with outbuildings and a good deal of forestation surrounding which exists today. However significant changes have occured with the building of a gate lodge to the right of entrance, loss of part of the main house building on the north eastern side and demolishment of all the out buildings to the north of the house. This has left only a walled outline enclosure which almost mirrors that on its eastern side, giving the impression of two side-by-side walled gardens. A part of the old building between the house and western garden remains and contains a window and fireplace hidden behind its camouflaging shrubbery. The house itself has functioned as a guest house since the 1960s and likely similar catering requirements placed on the kitchen as an orphanage in the late 19th century.

The eastern and original garden slopes naturally down to the north with a stream on that walls outside and the altered wall in the north east corner houses a small recess (14x11x7 inches) which is noted as a possible bee bole (see Bee Keeping). Discovery of slab covered stone drains running northwards confirm its active past drainage and south facing wall metal pegs also indicates past wall usage for fruit training.

Little current use is made of the enclosed area where soft fruit and some vegetables are sown and the adjacent west enclosure is principally neglected, but has elderly fruit trees (apple) and donkeys in residence.

Entrance east garden

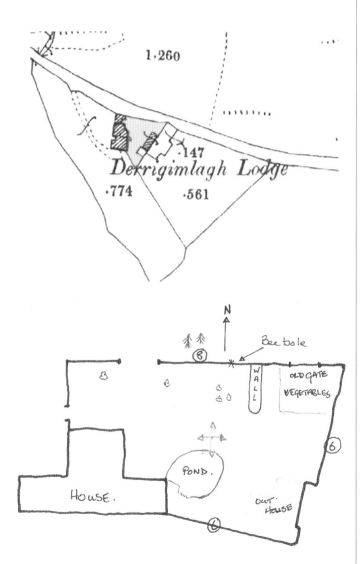

Derrigimlagh Lodge

A small building sits on this site on the 6 inch map but expands to a larger house with outbuildings on the 25 inch. Its history is obscure but the townland of Derrigimlagh sustained a mission school, was to have had one of Nimmos roads run to it from Ballynahinch, stood close to the Marconi station and the lodge was probably improved to the 25 inch map standard by Kendalls of Ardagh.

Today it has a small enclosing garden situated immediately on its eastern side with its highest wall on the north. This has a large arched gate and further east, a blocked up second gate site, along with a windowed wall on the east wall which incorporates a small outbuilding. Purchased from Faherty in 1974 the house has been extensively altered by the current owners (Halliday) who came across cobblestoned areas in the garden area. This, along with the two large gate sites, could add weight to the suggestion that horse and carriages (cars) may have used this yard. There is no known history of any significant walled kitchen garden for this area and today it provides a sheltered pleasurable garden, with pond and a small dedicated vegetable growing area.

Of note hidden behind ivy and a climbing rose on the northern wall is a small recess which is registered as a bee bole (see Bee Keeping).

Old gate

View SE to NW

Water feature or greenhouse

Garden bell

Water holding pond above garden

Townland: Kill
GPS: 53° 28' 51" N   10° 04' 08" W
Elevation: 24m
Protected Structure: Yes
Access: At main house

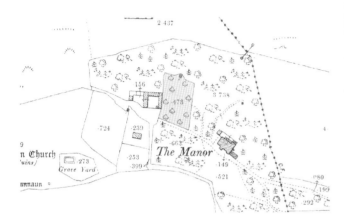

Errislannan Manor

This hunting lodge bought in 1840 by Rev Henry Wall, was extended in 1850 and his daughter married Rev George Heather in 1866 and their family members were subsequently in residence until sold to the late Dr Donald Brooks in 1958. His wife Stephanie continues to reside there, running the estate and equestrian centre.

The written history of this manor reflects the local history of events of the times, its occupants' involvement and their appreciation of their enviroment which established the goodwill the peninsula has extended to the manor's successive owners.

The walled garden is almost surrounded by sheltering trees, except for the outbuildings on its western boundary and rising hill beyond. These sheltering trees extend to the house but separate in front of the house to permit it oversee the lawn running down to the lake. The tree lined driveway with fields either side and a calm harbour behind all combine to make this peninsular location all things idyllic in Connemara country living.

Some 3,000 trees were planted in the 1840s (mainly sycamores, with occasional conifer) and the garden outside the northern wall has a ditch for water diversion. A small rectangular structure is seen on the inside of this wall on the 25 inch map, which may have been a holding pool for water or, according to Stephanie Brooks, a small greenhouse structure. Orchard planting is indicated on the 25 inch map within the walled garden with no formal pathways. The manor's vegetable planting diary of 1890 includes cucumbers which may have been grown in the main house's south eastern corners greenhouse addition and the remainder of vegetables, fruit and herbs coming from this garden. Flowers always featured in the garden's history either as ornamental for the house, church occasions or, for a period, export of daffodils to the Dublin market. Initially cattle and fowl and then ponies would have provided the manure source along with seaweed.

The gardens are now mainly ornamental with walk ways, herbaceous borders, some fruit trees of varying age and vegetable plantings on the west side along with a small modern greenhouse. A portion of the south east wall of the garden was knocked to allow for apple thief surveillance, then subsequently replaced by metal railings which in turn were later recycled for use in the dog kennels' whelping pen.

Townland:	Garraunbaun
GPS:	53° 33' 03" N 10° 01' 05" W
Elevation:	46m
Protected Structure:	No
Access:	Private

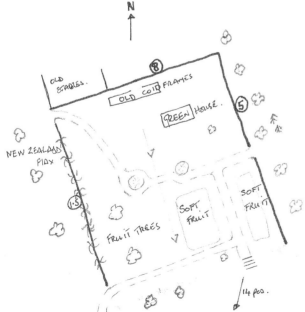

Garraunbaun House

Built in 1852 for Charles Palmer Archer (Lord Mayor of Dublin) the house ownership passed through the Duane and Lavelle families, followed by Col. Irwin before being renovated by its current owner Neil O'Donoghue in 2005.

The house's elevated south east position overlooking Ballinakill Harbour conceals its garden to the rear and on an incline down from the original stables (now in separate ownership). Judicious early tree planting on the western side gave resultant shelter.

This once enclosed garden has its western wall replaced by New Zealand flax and the southern wall is now a step down terrace to the house. The northern wall has been replaced with block and forms part of the stables perimeter with no evidence of greenhouse or wall plantings although a low frame outline may represent a one time cold frame. The eastern wall stonework is not the original save for the mortared stone gate pillars.

Although devoid of the original walled protection, its mature wood, remaining wall and position sandwiched between house and stable, does allow some wind buffering. Sufficient to protect some fruit trees, soft fruit and shrubs to provide the owner with a pleasant rear view and some garden produce.

West garden view S to N

East garden view W to E

Lime kiln

Townland:	Garroman
GPS:	53° 27' 34" N 9° 44' 49" W
Elevation:	37m
Protected Structure:	N/A
Access:	Private

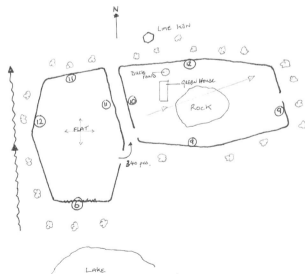

Glendolagh House

Subterranean kitchen entrance to demolished Glendolagh House

A native oak wood on the south side of lake Glendolagh, in an area he knew from fishing holidays, was the house building site chosen by a protestant clergyman, Dean Mahon from Westport in the 1830s. The 6 inch map confirms the site and also two large walled gardens (map characteristics indicating cultivated areas). Remarks by Robert Graham (of Redgorton, 1836) praises Mahon for his modern establishment of residence and gardens layout. Similarly W.H. Bartlett (*The Scenery and Antiquities of Ireland* circa 1841) refers to the then late Dean Mahon's great taste in his choice of place of abode. Subsequent owners, occupiers or lessors (Strutzers, Berridges, Mongans, Mannions, Nee, Prittie) must have enjoyed this lakeside situation, which in its hey-day had the two storey over basement house, and various later additions of turrets, battlements, adjacent farmyard and store with stables and hayloft just to the east. Following abandonement, fire and danger of collapse the building was demolished (1960) and the debris used to contstruct new housing and a road to the west.

The magnificently contstructed walled gardens, present since their initial build, remain virtually intact and are of a size disproportionate to the house and its demands, being only used as a hotel by the Mongan sisters in the 1940s. A living member of the domestic staff recalls 10 guest rooms in the hotel, the supply of vegetables from the garden, and the genteel clientel who enjoyed the peace and beauty.

The tall curved garden walls contour one another where they meet to enclose two individual areas of good size, but one flat (west) and the other (east) sloped with a large amount of surface area unusable, due to the stone that projects above the soil. Both are sheltered by surrounding woodlands which threaten the walls and where sheep are now enclosed in grassy meadowland. A not very old pear and apple tree survive in the west garden, where part of its south wall has been rebuilt to a lower level. Where the wall contours meet, two opposing gated openings, each built within their own high wall, remain. An elaborate lime kiln beside the gardens, uses the lands differing heights to facilitate the loading and flue formation.

The ambitious design, construction and size of these walled gardens but their absence of progressive improvements within them (a greenhouse, wall fixtures and a small duck pond date from the mid-20th century) suggests diminishing interest following their build and some mystery as to what they were built for in the first place.

View SW to NE

View S to N

Heated greenhouse remains

Exterior south wall with piers

Townland:	Pollacappul
GPS:	53º 33' 51" N 9º 54' 35" W
Elevation:	43m
Protected Structure:	Yes
Access:	Open

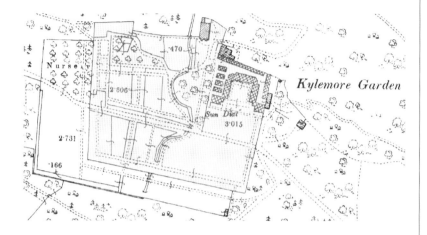

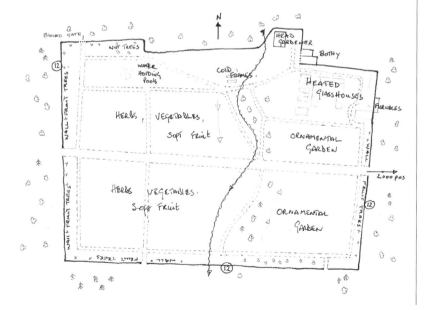

Kylemore Gardens

Dr Mitchell Henry bought the lands in 1862 and with professional help and vision set about building his iconic home and gardens. Exceptional in its concept , advanced for its time and place, affordable due to his wealth, he created artificial growing conditions to allow a wide variety of vegetables which included exotic fruits and plants. Formulated to plans evolving in western Europe for the Victorian walled garden, as the industrial revolution created suitable products and machinery. However, the death of his wife, loss of his fortune and retirement from politics led to the sale of Kylemore in 1903 to a Mr Zimmerman's (of Chicago) daughter (Duchess of Manchester). Following family acrimony the estate was sold to Ernest Fawke in 1914. The gardens suffered neglect and eventually in 1920 the Benedictine Nuns (from Ypres) bought the castle and estate as their new Abbey.

The walled garden contained pipework for water supply and electricity generation, holding pools for irrigation and a most ambitious arrangement of heated greenhouses to support amongst exotic fruit, vines, bananas, melons, flowers and probably pineapples. Outbuildings included a lime kiln, furnaces, a bothy and the head gardener's overseeing accommodation. A dedicated team would have been required to service this complex growing area to supply produce to the main house and also export to his other home in London.

Large arched entrance gates permitted passage of guests on foot or by carriage from the main house,through this formally laid out garden which was some distance from the house and amidst new forestry, river and lake.

The Benedictine Nuns careful progressive restoration of these gardens since 1995, is commendable and which now, amidst even more mature surroundings, still provokes surprise and delight to the discovering visitor as they pass through the gates.

West wall

Cold frames (circled) and garden holding pond

Water holding pond above house

Townland:	Kylemore
GPS:	53° 33' 49" N 9° 50' 27" W
Elevation:	43m
Protected Structure:	Yes
Access:	At guesthouse

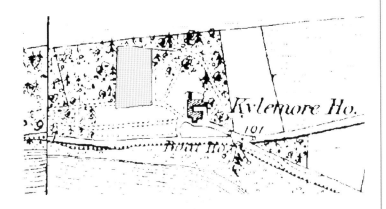

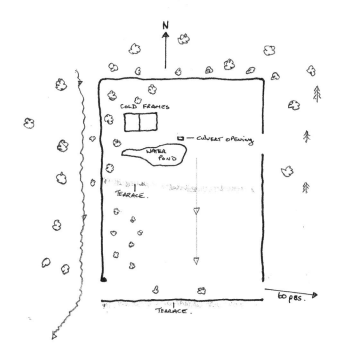

Kylemore House

Since the 1840s Rev Jos Duncan had a local presence as a landowner/lessor before Kylemore House was apparently built for him in 1853. He subsequently operated it as a lakeside hotel for sportsmen and was actively involved in local food rights and the auxillary workhouse during the great famine.

Occupants/owners since then include Andrew Armstrong (ran the house as a hotel), Lord Ardilaun (reverted to private house) Talbot Clifton (as a home) St John Gogarty (as a temporary home following Renvyle fire) Gazby as a home (an Englishman on his retirement from China where he practised law) until its current owner Nancy Naughton, who has run it as a guest house since 1973.

The garden is a short distance from the house but with low walls and slopes in two gentle terraces down to the passing lakeside main road. A stream runs just outside the west wall. The remains of two (each 4ftx10ft) cement sided probable cold frames remain in the upper west side of garden with a small 2ft deep pit in front which has a culvert opening into it from above. This was likely a water holding pool with the water diverted above from the stream to the west. However, a larger holding pool is located above and to the east of the house.

The house's history should have placed a deal of necessity and interest for food production and the storage pool and cold frames would suggest this, but recent local oral history only recalls some residual plum and apple trees with any vegetable production succumbing to supply from other sources.

The garden is heavily overgrown with laurel, rhododendron, opportunistic and fallen trees, barely restrained by the disintegrating dry stonewalls and all indicative of long lost activity and interest in the garden. There is no current usage for garden produce, but some use has been made of it as an obstacle course for the non-fishing hotel guests.

View W to E

Water pipe in path

Townland:	Letterdyfe
GPS:	53° 24' 29" N 9° 55' 12" W
Elevation:	23m
Protected Structure:	Yes
Access:	Private

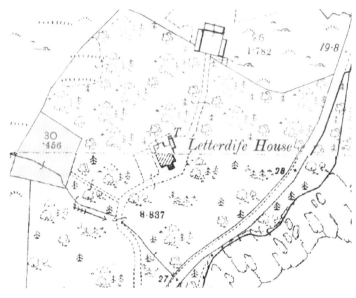

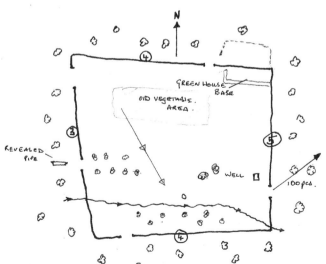

Letterdyfe House

Letterdyfe house along with significant outbuildings to the north-east were built as a private residence for the land agent George Robinson in the mid-1880s. His son's (Henry) youngest daughter and successive owner, Olive, later changed the house to the style of a guest house and thereafter a Dutch consortium bought the estate in 1965 and has made no significant changes to it, their interest being mainly botanical.

This small estate now lies in a surprisingly heavily wooded area just outside and to the east of Roundstone. It is sheltered by a ground rise to its west and locally dense tree planting. The finely built two-storey outbuildings are not used and their orifaces blocked for preservation.

The walled garden is enclosed within mainly low walls and contains a stream, spring well and remains of a greenhouse base and wall, the interior of which is rendered. A surface portion of a cast iron pipe bringing water from an upper damned portion of the stream reveals itself above the west wall. A 20th century addition of a tennis court, now overgrown, is on the outside of the north east portion of the

garden and the changing room reported to have been behind the greenhouse wall. The clear, wandering, stone-edged, moss-covered pathways and trees soften the walk through this garden in which seasonal floral carpets and naturally organised self-seeded trees have long since replaced the vegetables, soft fruit and fruit trees. An acceptable exchange for the majority, but one which would not perhaps have been tolerated by its first owner.

Townland: Ballinafad
GPS: 53° 27' 33" N 9° 48' 44" W
Elevation:
Protected Structure: Yes
Access: Private

Lisnabruka

In 1910 Willcox (USA) took this house build on as a project with an inheritance and a like of fishing in this area. Built as a substantial home with views over the eastern end of Ballynahinch lake it had no 'real' walled garden. A particulary colourful spring garden on its south facing 'Barclays bank' does however have a low retaining stone wall running along it with mid-way the remains of a furnace heated greenhouse. A local gardener remembers it being used for seed propagation and supporting a fig tree, with vegetables grown in the ground area just in front of the greenhouse.

The house remains in family ownership through Willcox's daughter, Mrs Reid, who occupies it periodically and has also been rented to and enjoyed by many summer holiday groups.

No walled garden possibly because the owner always felt it was too windy despite his tree planting, or simply built in a time when garden produce became more readily available and gardeners more expensive.

Furnace and greenhouse remains

View SE to NW

Ice house or smokehouse, interior view

Ice house or smoke house exterior

NE corner of remaining main garden walls

Well

View E to W (arena)

Townland:	Ardbear
GPS:	53° 28' 57" N 10° 01' 46" W
Elevation:	16m
Protected Structure:	Yes
Access:	At guesthouse

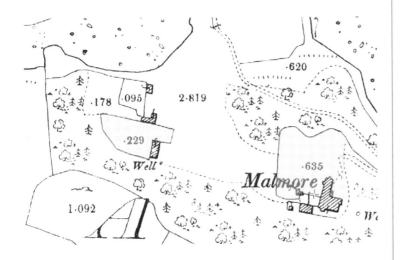

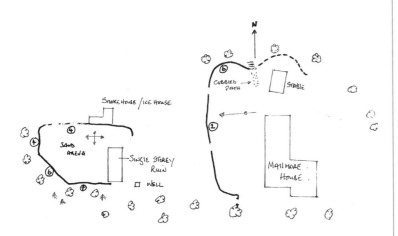

Mallmore

The acres on the south side of the Clifden estuary where it narrows into the harbour, offers shelter, views of the bay to the west and eventually Clifden town to the north-east along with shoreline access. Optimal conditions for a house near a 'commercial centre' and taken advantage of by early buildings noted on the 6 inch map. However, it was not apparently until 1864 that James D'Arcy built the more substantive house for his home on land from his brother John. Subsequent owners/occupiers were: Bishop O'Sullivan (his legacy an elevated seat overlooking the bay . . . the bishop's chair), Retired Col Brown 1920s (his legacy as a plantsman included rhododendrons from Kew gardens, pollarded lime tree), Cubbins, O'Toole, Connolly, McEvaddy and currently Hardman, the latter having managed Mallmore as a guest house since 1980.

Walled garden remains are as per those associated with D'Arcy's Mallmore house (6 inch map) but not enclosing. They are changed today with only a high element of wall remaining on the north with a stepped down break to a lower level rose garden and that on the west altered to leave now only a low-based garden retaining wall, which appears sensible in order not to block the westerly attractive view. Today the garden has ornamental planting, a pond and some young fruit trees, reverting to its likely original use as a pleasure garden for the house guests.

The old ruin to the west was a large solid single storey residential building beside a level low walled area which in the recent past contained cement cold frames, but is now a sand arena. The rising ground to its south west and eastern approach has a well established mixture of mature trees. This may have been the Coneys' or even John D'Arcy senior's early 18th century Connemara residence.

Immediately beside this ruin is a stone enclosed spring well with linteled ope and limestone table. Lower down towards the shore line is a well constructed smaller building built into the side of the rising ground, which, without invasive investigation, must be considered to be either a smoke house or an ice house and may have had some connection with the larger building beside it. This combination might have been a fish curing station.

It is likely then that the garden produce area was at the earlier and more protected western site (arena now) which did have an associated orchard and now a small modern greenhouse. Today's kitchen garden requirements are met from discreet growing beds beside the new and within the older walled garden areas.

Townland:	Ardbear
GPS:	53° 28' 37" N 10° 01' 42" W
Elevation:	17m
Protected Structure:	Yes
Access:	Private

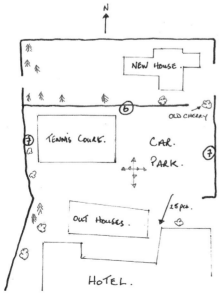

Rock Glen Hotel

Possibly a speculative build by John Reville in 1825 (employed by Nimmo as a pay clerk but had an eye for a building site) as he sold shortly after to Major Digby. A succession of occupants followed: Scully (agent of Eyre family), Lyons (building changes), then an ownership void until Dr Pit Gorham 1880s, Fannins 1930, Hawksley 1950, Roche 1972, Conneely 2004.

Although originating as a modest house it had a number of significant alterations/extensions made during the tenancies of Lyons and Roche evolving as a well known hotel with 27 guest rooms, extensive grounds and staff accommodation. It lost its forge, carriage room, gardener's cottage, animal housing and lastly its walled gardens which were sacrificed to facilitate guest parking, tennis court and a managers house.

The two walled areas seen on the 25 inch map were used as a source of garden produce and for animal husbandry certainly in the late 1800s but with the conversion from private residency to guest house (Hawksley) then Hotel (Roche) garden produce must have been progressively outsourced. However living memory recalls the kitchen using its garden resources in their menus and strawberries for their renowned strawberry and cream afternoon teas. Water (well in front and later water piped from Faul lake) and manure sources readily available with good tree shelter from the south and south west and conifers within the western border. The two old cherry blossom trees give testament to the resultant shelter.

The walls, some removed where new entrances were made, are covered with ivy, the ground in tarmac and a few of their previous inmates appearing at the edge of the tarmac (oregano) or in the hedges (raspberry). The paddock garden contains the managers house with its own overgrowing new garden.

Sadly and to the dissappointment of those locals, golfers, tourists and painters that enjoyed the location, tranquillity, hospitality and food, the hotel at the time of writing is no longer operational.

Site of original walled garden

Well

Most southerly garden

Garden sea walls

<table>
<tr><td>Townland:</td><td>Ervellagh</td></tr>
<tr><td>GPS:</td><td>53° 23' 23" N 9° 55' 04" W</td></tr>
<tr><td>Elevation:</td><td>9m</td></tr>
<tr><td>Protected Structure:</td><td>Part only</td></tr>
<tr><td>Access:</td><td>Open</td></tr>
</table>

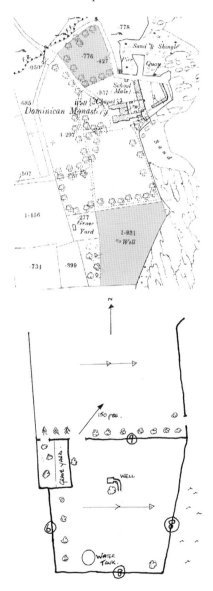

Roundstone Monastery

The Roundstone Franciscan monastery was established (1835) in a similar fashion to Clifden in that the brothers presence commenced in a house and small church locally (Roundstone) until they bought a detached house (1848, Seaville Lodge) on the shore line. They built accommodation, chapel and school along with a farm, orchard and vegetable section within their walls. The extensive walled area of the monastery commenced at the gated northern entrance, ran along the shore line of the eastern

side continuing across the south, up the west side to complete the enclosure at the northern gates.

The original walled garden was immediately inside the gates on the left where fruit trees grew and vegetables were sown but this area was replaced when the complex was demolished and the new school built.

Other walled areas for garden produce and animal husbandry were the two most southerly enclosures, both sloping down to the sea. There is a spring well on the most southerly and the monastery graveyard lies above on its western side. The walls on this enclosure offer the only shelter from the predominant weather front, whilst in the other, border planting of sycamore trees lends some shelter or shade for animals.

Local historians recall the brothers produce being sold in the village throughout their occupation and no doubt they would have also played their part in food assistance during the lean famine years as well as a role similar to that of the Clifden Monastery in providing food for attending school children.

Today only the bell tower, entrance gates, graveyard and the western, southern and part of the eastern walls remain, as the complex was demolished in 1979 for the IDA (now Killeen) Business Park. An established national school and private housing replaces the monastery, its outbuildings and vegetable garden. The impressive seaward walls of the southerly garden areas remain intact and in good order, the enclosed land is regulary grazed so kept "clean" and remains hardly disturbed by human footfall in this secluded part of the park.

View SE to NW

Townland:	Shanboolard
GPS:	53° 33' 43" N 10° 03' 34" W
Elevation:	42 m
Protected Structure:	No
Access:	Private

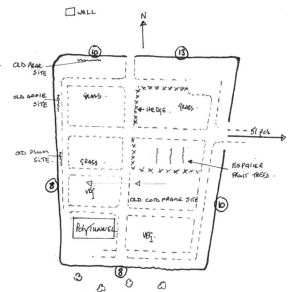

Shanboolard

With land bought from the Martin Estate in 1849 Edward Whitwell probably built and certainly lived in this house in the 1850s which changed hands to Acheson in the 1860s before William Armstrong bought it in 1890. (A conditional monetary gift aided this purchase provided the Armstrongs took on their benefactors name of Tulloch). Following William's (1901) and Kathleen's second husband's death (1905), she continued to live there until a son, Kinmont and daughter-in-law Doris (sister of Olive Robinson, Letterdyfe) came to manage the house and she moved to Cartron House where she died in 1938. Graham Tulloch (Kinmont and Doris's son) inherited and managed Shanboolard until his death in 1990, when Ashley Mathews pruchased and commenced it's reconditioning.

This is one of the higher exposed gardens viewed and one of the very few surviving in its original function. It appears a well-planned and attended property having had evolving technology applied during its development. Acheson's financial injection, followed by the interest of the formidable pony and garden loving Kathleen Armstrong-Lushington-Tulloch resulted, for example, in extensive outbuildings, piped water from holding tanks, electricity generated from wind, orchard and underfloor heated greenhouses. The latter which stood between the house and walled garden were blown away by hurricanc Debbie (1961), and the apple orchard has also not survived.

The westward, slightly sloping walled garden lies very comfortably beside and just below the house with an ornamental garden interveening. The stone for the mortared walls came from the quarry within the domain and is rendered on the south facing wall only. A tree shelter belt exists but mainly to the south, which leaves the west wall the only exposure protection as the bare land below it slopes down to stream and shore. All walls are in good state and its current owner maintains an active interest in the gardens use by the installation and growing of all season produce in a polytunnel, maintaining the pathways between ordered beds of vegetables, soft fruit and fanned fruit, whilst keeping bees outside the garden.

View E to N

Stone supported terrace

Base outline of greenhouse in front of south facing wall

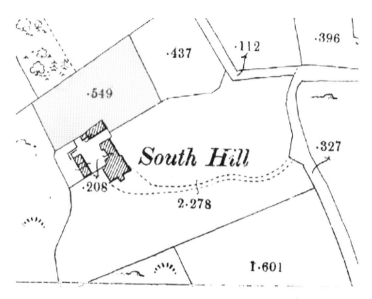

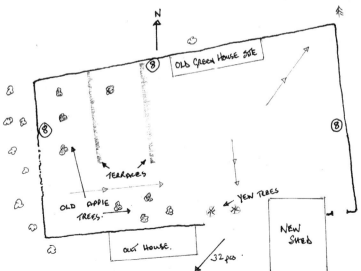

South Hill

Southhill was built on a plot of D'Arcy ground given by Hyacinth to his sister Elizabeth on her marriage to Lt George Clarke c1850. Sold to Alexander Dickson in 1858, he enlarged this small lodge and lived there up untill 1877 when he sold to Joseph Goreham. Gerard Stanley bought the house in 1921 from Gorham's sister (King), and housed his drapery shop apprentices here. The local Mulkerrin brothers tended the garden and land until residency was taken up by Kevin Stanley (1965) whose family remain in the house.

Encircling high walls, natural shelter, drainage, proximity to the house and the presence of outhouses, provided all the necessary constituents to function as a kitchen fruit and vegetable garden. The protective hill to the west drops down to the garden which has two stone supported terraces in its western section and still holds some old fruit trees. On the northern wall on its eastern side the solid base outline of a mid-20th century greenhouse remains with rendering on its associated wall. Tomatoes and vines were known to be grown in this and the same owner kept honey bees.

The garden wall capping, always thought to contain glass fragments, was presumably a deterrent to orchard raiding.

The Stanley family were productive gardeners supplying Clifden and the Rock Glen hotel with produce and other associated land on the property industriously worked in soft fruit and livestock. Here at one time 3,000 hens kept Clifden (and Galway in the out of tourist season) supplied with eggs, until the hen houses were converted into greenhouses in the late 20th century.

The garden is now fallow with some control of overgrowth delegated to a few sheep.

Entrance to garden

Townland:	Streamstown
GPS:	53° 30' 42" N 10° 02' 38" W
Elevation:	20m
Protected Structure:	Yes
Access:	Private

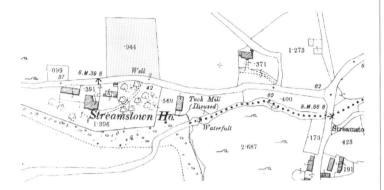

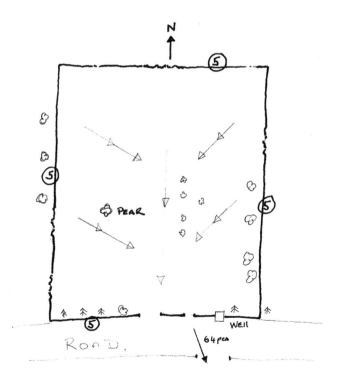

Streamstown House

This shoreside house location situated beside a river outlet at the head of Streamstown Bay, was granted under the Act of Settlement to the Coneys and has remained in the their family possesion since then. They have frequent mention in local history and were principally farmers of a large acerage with another family branch in Ardbear. The 6 inch map records the Streamstown house and a number of out buildings, the house having had enlargement since then. Identified to the east in this map is a Tuck mill (used to finish woven cloth) but prefixed as disused in the 25 inch map and later demolished in the 1960s. A large corn store still stands immediately west of the house. This was therefore a diverse site of industry with additional family related interests situated elsewhere.

Behind the house across the road is, on the 25 inch map, a marked area of land which rises sharply to the northern, eastern and western sides. It is enclosed by a lowish dry stone wall with mature trees standing inside (east and south) and outside (west) its boundaries, which, combined, create a minuture sheltered valley sloping down to the south. The walls have some parts of disrepair and have only one smallish old entrance in the south wall visible today (the larger one nearby is recent), and the old well is incorporated in this wall. An original large gate was probably lost and the well became part of the boundary wall when a strip of land was taken to make the road shown in the 25 inch map.

The 6 inch map helps confirm this as a cultivated area by characterising a larger orderly planted area which conforms to its smaller current shape and size by simple division with another stone wall.

The current Coneys occupant recalls fruit trees growing in here along with vegetables. Inside this garden a scattered growth of blackthorn easily survives along with a single old falling pear tree but which only produces annual leaf growth. The land is intermittently used for livestock grazing and would require some caution for machine cultivation, due to its gradient.

View NW to SE

Townland: Cashel
GPS: 53° 24'57" N 9° 47' 41" W
Elevation: 16 m
Protected Structure: Yes
Access: At hotel

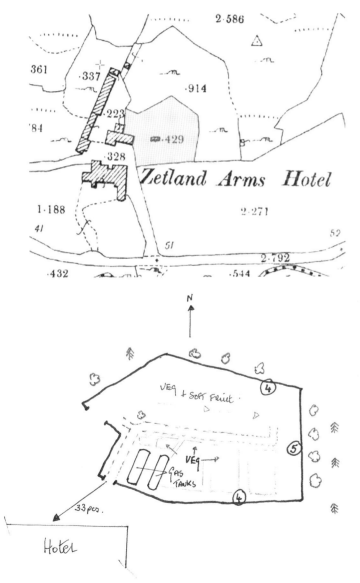

Zetland Hotel

Cashel Bay was an early coastal shipping destination for trading and the house built by O'Loughlin c1850, himself a merchant and trader, took on the role of guest house when his daughter assumed control. A visit by the Viceroy established its hospitality and trading position in Connemara and subsequent owners (Guinness company/family, Toohy, Scaflo, Prendergast and currently Redmond) continued its hospitality role by increasing guest and staff accommodation.

Above and behind the hotel water was piped down from initially a dam and later holding tanks. The pipes traversed the walled garden which was low walled perhaps because of its sheltered mini-valley site and natural drainage with no significant (or necessary) shelter belt planting. Some of the south western wall was moved inwards to allow installation of petrol storage tanks. The "absence of significant tree planting surrounding these dry stone walls means that the garden entrance gives the impression of an original, conveniently placed, inexpensive, suitable vegetable growing area, unlike many others of dedicated construction.

The many outbuildings within past living memory housed ponies, cattle, sheep, pigs and hens all for hotel use, but are now redundant.

Recent tillage of this garden has revealed indications of its application with findings of gravel drainage channels, the old traversing water pipes, path edgings and fertile soil. The contemporary local historians recall its all seasonal production of vegetables consumed by the hotel guests. The garden, because of this fairly continuous usage, has not deteriorated into a totally overgrown state and has not hindered the current owners renewed interest in its potential for reclamation.

Useful references

These written observations assume some knowledge of the topography, demography and history of Connemara. For those not familar with them or wish more detail, I have listed a number of reference articles/books used, the majority of which are the excellent research work of local authors and are readily available.

Kathleen Villiers-Tuthill:	*Beyond the Twelve Bens*	
	Patient Endurance	ISBN 0 9530455 0 1
	History of Clifden 1810-1860	....
	Alexander Nimmo	ISBN 0-9530455-3-6
	History of Kylemore Castle and Abbey	ISBN 0-9542310-1-5
	A Colony of Strangers	ISBN 978-0-9530455-6-3
Tim Robinson: Connemara trilogy:	*Listening to the Wind*	ISBN-13: 978-1-844-88065-2, ISBN-10; 1-844-88065-2
	The Last Pool of Darkness	ISBN 978-1-844-88155-0
	A Little Gaelic Kingdom	ISBN 978-1-844-88237-3
Tim Robinson:	*Connemara Map and Gazetteer*	ISBN 0 9504002 5 4
Tully Cross Guild ICA;	*Portrait of a Parish*	
Thomas Colville Scott:	*Connemara After the Famine*	Published (1995) by The Lilliput Press Ltd
Henry Heaney (Editor)	*The Irish Journals of Robert Graham of Redgorton*	ISBN 1-85182-454-5
Eibhlin Ní Scannlain:	*Land and People*	ISBN 0 9517138 33
Breandan O Scanaill:	*Historical Sketchbook*	ISBN 978-0-9554146-1-9
Peter Somerville-Large	*The Irish Country House: A Social History*	ISBN 1-85619-237-7
Neville Figgis (Editor)	*A Clifden Anthology*	ISBN 978-0-9571848-0-0

The reader may also find these web sites of help:

Protected Structures Galway County:	www.galway.ie/en/Services/Conservation/RecordofProtectedStructures
Ordnance Survey Ireland:	www.maps.osi.ie/publicviewer
Landed Estates:	www.landedestates.ie/NUI Galway
Google Earth:	www.googleearth.com
National Archives Census of Ireland 1901/11:	www.census.nationalarchives.ie/
A Statistical And Agricultural Survey of The County of Galway by Hely Dutton :	www.aughty-org/pdf/county_galway_dutton.pdf
Climate Change – Refining the Impacts for Ireland:	http://www.epa.ie/downloads/pubs/research/climate/name,26008,en.html